La Conquistadora

The Story of the Oldest Statue of the Virgin Mary
in the United States

Map of *El Camino Real de Tierra Adentro* (Royal Road of the Interior) from Mexico City to Santa Fe. This 1600-mile trade route was designated a National Historic Trail in 2000.

La Conquistadora

The Story of the Oldest Statue of the Virgin Mary
in the United States

Sue Houser

SUNSTONE PRESS
SANTA FE

© 2011 by Sue Houser.
All Rights Reserved.

No part of this book may be reproduced in any form or by any electronic or mechanical means including information storage and retrieval systems without permission in writing from the publisher, except by a reviewer who may quote brief passages in a review.

Sunstone books may be purchased for educational, business, or sales promotional use. For information please write: Special Markets Department, Sunstone Press, P.O. Box 2321, Santa Fe, New Mexico 87504-2321.

Book and Cover design › Vicki Ahl
Body typeface › Lucida Bright
Printed on acid free paper

Library of Congress Cataloging-in-Publication Data

Houser, Sue.
  La Conquistadora : the story of the oldest statue of the Virgin Mary in the United States / Sue Houser.
    p. cm.
  Chapter titles in English and Spanish.
  Includes bibliographical references.
  ISBN 978-0-86534-830-1 (softcover : alk. paper)
 1. Conquistadora. 2. Mary, Blessed Virgin, Saint--Devotion to--New Mexico--Santa Fe. 3. Catholic Church--New Mexico--Santa Fe--History. 4. Santa Fe (N.M.)--Church history. I. Title.
  BT660.S45H68 2011
  247--dc23
                    2011027203

WWW.SUNSTONEPRESS.COM
SUNSTONE PRESS / POST OFFICE BOX 2321 / SANTA FE, NM 87504-2321 / USA
(505) 988-4418 / ORDERS ONLY (800) 243-5644 / FAX (505) 988-1025

Contents

Preface —— 7
Acknowledgments —— 11

El Descubrimiento de la Estatua —— 13
Discovery of the Statue

Los que Vinieron Antes —— 17
Those Who Came Before

La Vida en Nuevo México —— 21
Life in New Mexico

La Revuelta Indígena —— 27
The Indians Revolt

Regresando a Casa —— 31
Returning Home

La Restauración —— 47
The Restoration

Nombres Nuevos —— 51
New Names

La Capilla de La Conquistadora —— 53
La Conquistadora Chapel

El Guardarropa y las Joyas de la Reina —— 57
The Queen's Wardrobe and Jewelry

El Secuestro —— 73
The Kidnapping

La Fiesta de Santa Fe —— 77
The Santa Fe Fiesta

La Procesión a Rosario —— 81
Procession to Rosario

Bibliography —— 91

Preface

My first encounter with *La Conquistadora* was when I walked in the procession to Rosario Chapel with my friend, Mary. We joined other pilgrims, singing, chanting, and praying behind elegantly dressed *caballeros* shouldering a platform that held the regal-looking statue. Upon reaching the small adobe chapel, we knelt on bare tile floors and continued singing, chanting, and praying.

Until then, I did not know that *La Conquistadora* is the oldest statue of the Virgin Mary in the United States, that she came here with the Spanish colonists, or that she has a wardrobe suitable for a queen. I was touched by the devotion given this small wooden statue and became intrigued with her story.

My first inclination was to write about her amazing wardrobe of over 200 dresses. However, my walk in the procession was an extraordinary experience—being part of a tradition based on a promise made and kept for over 300 years. I also considered focusing on the settlement of New Mexico, but it is well documented, for which I am grateful.

I decided to weave a story highlighting the devotion to *La Conquistadora,* a devotion that has sustained people for centuries and inspired rituals and traditions. I wanted to introduce the statue to people who, like me, may not know her story.

This book briefly chronicles the discovery of the humble statue in Mexico City, her tragedies and triumphs, and her rise to the throne as Queen of New Mexico. Spanish subtitles remind readers of *La Conquistadora's* important relationship with early settlers and of the connection between present-day celebrations and traditions that are rooted in the Spanish Colonial Era. The book contains historical and contemporary photographs as well as color photographs taken of her wardrobe.

While working on the manuscript, I glimpsed into *La Conquistadora's* closet and met with *sacristanas* who shared their personal experiences of sewing for her and attending to her. I traced the steps of Fiesta attendees to the Cross of the Martyrs, scanned old newspapers on microfiche, attended the inaugural "Fabric of Our Faith" exhibit at the cathedral, and visited the Museum of Spanish Colonial Art and *El Rancho de las Golondrinas*, a Spanish Colonial Living History Museum. In my frequent travels to Northern New Mexico, the La Conquistadora Chapel in Santa Fe is now a regular stop.

La Conquistadora captured my heart as she has done with many other New Mexicans and people around the world. She may capture your heart as well.

Acknowledgments

I want to thank my Catholic friend, Mary Diecker, for introducing me to *La Conquistadora* and for her patience in explaining religious traditions and language that were foreign to me; *Sacristana* Terry Garcia and former *sacristanas*, Mary Martinez-Dean and Emelda Martinez-Garcia, for sharing their personal stories related to the sacred statue; Larry Greenly and Roger Blake for bringing the story to life with photographs; my writing friends, Wendy, Jackie, Rob, Larry, and Nadine, who tirelessly supported my tenacious pursuit of this project; my niece, April, for technical support; Larry and Susan for their encouragement; and my husband, Roger, for the many trips to Santa Fe. May *La Conquistadora* bless you all.

El Descubrimiento de la Estatua
Discovery of the Statue

The year was 1623. Fray Alonso de Benavides, a priest in Mexico City, received a special assignment to establish missions in the kingdom of *Nuevo México*, now known as New Mexico. While searching for altar cloths, chalices, and vestments to furnish the new parishes, he opened a box in a dusty warehouse and discovered a beautiful hand-carved statue of the Virgin Mary. The wooden form resembled a Moorish princess. Her plastered garments were painted crimson and covered in gold leaf with tiny arabesques of red, orange, and blue. Her wooden base was carved into a cloud with the faces of three happy cherubs.

"Where did this precious image of the Virgin Mary come from?" asked Father Benavides.

People shrugged. Some said she must have come from the Old World. They could imagine a woodcutter chopping down trees to heat his humble home and discovering, in a single log, an image resembling the Virgin Mary. The woodcarver would have gently carved the image from the wood and, perhaps with the help of his wife, draped the statue in fabrics, which they plastered and painted. They might have summoned a local priest to bless the wooden symbol of their faith, thanking the Virgin Mary for allowing her image to be revealed in a piece of firewood.

"How could she have traveled across the oceans? Who brought her here?"

The priest's questions had no answers, but everyone agreed that the simple statue would be the perfect representation of the Virgin Mary in the new frontier. Since the native Indians already practiced a mystical religion, the statue might be helpful in converting them to Christianity. And, as one who had suffered and made sacrifices, the image of Mary would be a comforting presence to the *vecinos*, or settlers, who had left the security of Spain and Mexico to colonize a remote, harsh territory.

In time, a caravan left Mexico City and headed north to the new territory. Soldiers escorted a new governor for the kingdom, Felipe Sotelo, along with his servants.

Father Benavides and other missionaries traveled with them. Some went on horseback, some on burros, and some on foot. Oxen pulled two-wheeled, wooden carts carrying supplies. One cart contained a small altar, a crucifix, and the carefully packed wooden statue that Father Benavides had named *Nuestra Señora de La Asunción,* Our Lady of the Assumption, which was the name of an existing parish in the new kingdom.

Their first stop was at the Hill of Tepeyac, just north of Mexico City. This was the site where another image of the Virgin Mary, *Nuestra Señora de Guadalupe* or Our Lady of Guadalupe, had miraculously appeared to a simple peasant named Juan Diego in 1531. Subsequently, a church had been built at that location.

Everyone, from the oxcart drivers to the governor, paid a last visit to Our Lady of Guadalupe and asked for her protection on the journey to this unfamiliar region.

The procession trudged through bustling cities and mining towns, across green valleys and long stretches of parched desert. They forded rivers and climbed rugged mountains. Toward the end of the journey, they passed by multi-storied Indian villages and sprawling haciendas.

Los que Vinieron Antes
Those Who Came Before

The 1625 expedition was not the first to explore this region.

Rumors of the seven cities of gold had spurred Spain's interest in the New World. The Spaniards had driven the Moors out of their own country, and they were ready to conquer more lands. In 1492, King Ferdinand and Queen Isabella granted permission to Christopher Columbus to embark on a voyage to the Americas. Thereafter, colonies sprang up in what is today Florida, Puerto Rico, Cuba, and Mexico. However, as rumors go, searching for riches was elusive—the gold was always farther to the south or farther to the north.

In the early 1500s, some Europeans who reached the Americas had shipwrecked off the coast of what is now the state of Texas. They traveled on foot through the Southwest and saw what they believed to be cities of gold. It may have been that, from a distance, the straw and mud houses bathed in sunset resembled buildings shimmering in gold-toned brilliance. They headed south to Mexico, relating stories of riches and generating even more expeditions.

In 1540, Vasquez de Coronado headed a large expedition of soldiers seeking gold and priests seeking souls. They also brought sheep and horses, the first the Indians had seen. Coronado and his men followed rumors and explored the area of New Mexico and its various Indian pueblos. Finally, in 1542, Coronado's expedition packed up and returned empty-handed to Mexico City. Only a few zealous missionaries stayed behind.

The missionaries probably told the Pueblo Indians about the power in the Christian religion and about Juan Diego, a poor Indian in Mexico. He had been visited by a vision of a lady while on his way to church to pray for his seriously ill uncle. The lady called Juan by name and instructed him to ask the bishop to build her a church. The bishop doubted Juan Diego's story and sent him away. At the next encounter of the lady vision, Juan Diego told her the bishop wanted proof of her appearance. The lady showed him a garden of roses in full bloom, in spite of it being wintertime, and gave Juan Diego an armful of flowers. When Juan approached the bishop and opened his cloak, roses fell to the ground. The bishop saw, on the inside of Juan's cloak, an imprint of the heavenly image just as Juan had described. He immediately agreed to build the church she had requested. Juan Diego returned home to find that a vision of the same lady had visited his uncle, and he had been healed.

For the next 200 years, priests accompanied many expeditions into the Southwest. One expedition was led by Antonio de Espejo and Fray Bernaldino Beltrán. In Espejo's report, he gave the remote Spanish colonial outposts the name *Nuevo México,* which became the official name. He wrote that the Indians were rich in history and culture but not in gold.

Don Juan de Oñate, a native of New Spain, led another early expedition. His four-mile-long caravan included 129 soldiers, 250 *vecinos*, or settlers, and 10 Franciscan missionaries. They left Mexico carrying both the royal flag of the Spanish crown and the banner of the Catholic Church. In 1598, Oñate located a wide fertile valley and established the first colony, *San Juan de los Caballeros,* then later moved to *San Gabriel del Yunque.* However, Oñate disobeyed orders to treat the Indians in a civil manner and committed atrocities upon them. He was recalled to Mexico City where he was tried for improper treatment of the Indians and found guilty.

The Viceroy of New Spain appointed Pedro de Peralta to replace Oñate, and, in 1610, Peralta moved the settlement a few miles south. He established a new capital city at the base of the Sangre de Cristo Mountains and called it *La Villa Real de la Santa Fe*.

For a number of years, *Nuevo México* received little attention. Then the King of Spain heard of the Indians along the Rio Grande who had been Christianized and thousands more that needed to be. He decided *Nuevo México* should become a permanent settlement. By 1625, more than 50 churches had been built.

La Vida en Nuevo México
Life in New Mexico

Finally, in December 1625, the caravan carrying the sacred statue arrived at the headquarters for all the missions, Santo Domingo Pueblo. The travelers were enthusiastically welcomed since supplies came by wagon train only every three years.

Supplies were unloaded, and Governor Sotelo, Captain Gomez, and others continued on to Santa Fe, taking with them the lurching cart that carried religious items, including Our Lady of the Assumption.

Father Benavides stayed behind to put things in order and give the new governor time to get settled. A month later, Father Benavides went to Santa Fe where he was honored at a reception as the new head of the missions and delegate of the Holy Office. A mass was chanted at the Church of the Assumption. However, the parish church had been neglected, and Father Benavides considered it unfit for the Mother of God. He rallied the people to build a new church with a special place for Our Lady of the Assumption. Many people came to receive a blessing from her: the Spanish colonists, the Pueblo Indians, and even Apache war chiefs from the Plains. The unassuming statue welcomed everyone.

Before long, Father Benavides received another assignment. His services were needed elsewhere, so he bade farewell to the people of Santa Fe and to the statue that had traveled with him all the way from Mexico City.

The colonists adored the wooden representation of the Virgin Mary. She brought a soft, feminine presence to the colonists who were homesick for their families, churches and governments far away in Mexico and Spain. Members of the Confraternity of the Immaculate Conception, a religious order dedicated to taking care of the statue, promised Father Benavides they would honor and cherish her. After all, it was their religion that sustained them through all the hardships and challenges of settling in a foreign land.

They already adhered to the customs of the Old World by observing feast days with evening prayer services called vespers, which included singing, chanting and responsive readings. And, during processions through the streets, they sang hymns and offered prayers. Once the statue arrived, they carried the wooden image in their processions that wound through the dusty streets of Santa Fe.

To embellish their fiestas, religious celebrations, and even some processions, the colonists instigated an old custom from both Spain and Mexico of lighting little fires called *luminarias*, meaning "festival lanterns." The first *luminarias* in the new frontier were stacks of piñon wood laid criss-cross with kindling in the center. They were arranged around the homes and along the streets.

However, the pioneering women wanted hanging lanterns that would lend a romantic glow to the fiestas. So when the supply train from Mexico brought dishes wrapped in silk-like paper, the inventive women created *luminarias*, resembling Chinese lanterns. However, they were too fragile to hang, so the women shaped the colorful paper into lanterns, stuck a candle in the bottom with a handful of sand, and placed them on the flat roofs and walls. Later, when traders from the east brought goods in brown paper sacks, the sturdy sacks replaced the flimsy paper. These festive brown bags with flickering candles were a symbol for guiding the faithful, as well as welcoming the Christ Child and the statue of the Virgin Mary.

In addition to their customs and traditions, the Spaniards brought with them centuries of Arabic-Moorish influence on culture and lifestyle. The Moors had taught them to make mud bricks called *at-tub* in Arabic, or *adobe* in Spanish. Until then, the Indians' method of building mud houses was to place handfuls of wet adobe between two rows of poles or mix adobe with small rocks, letting it dry and then adding on another layer, handful by handful. The colonists also taught the Indians how to build and use *hornos*, outdoor beehive-shaped ovens made of *adobe*, which they had also learned from the Muslims. The Indians already had a method of irrigated farming, but the Spaniards taught them a more efficient method by building canals.

The Indians shared their resources of buckskin, corn, potatoes, squash, and herbs. The natives and newcomers combined pottery and weaving styles.

However, the Spanish missionaries imposed their religion on the Indians. They insisted that the Indians had a sinful nature and their salvation required them to believe in the Christian God. Many Indians converted. However, others maintained their ancient beliefs in the unity of nature, plants, and animals and continued to perform ceremonial dances, wear masks, and sprinkle sacred cornmeal. Tensions rose between the colonists and Indians, and they became fearful of one another.

The colonists remembered that when enemy forces in the Old World had threatened their ancestors, the Spaniards had marched through the streets and prayed for victory to Our Lady of the Rosary. Their attackers had been defeated. So the colonists followed their ancestors' example. They renamed their statue *Nuestra Señora del Santa Rosario*, Our Lady of the Rosary, and prayed for a peaceful co-existence with the Indians.

Another custom of the Old World was to dress images of the Virgin Mary in fine fabrics. However, Our Lady was a one-piece chunky block of wood not suitable for gowns of silks and satins, so woodworkers remade her wooden form. Arms were hacked away, iron hooks hammered into her shoulders, and moveable arms attached. They drilled holes through her earlobes. Her body was trimmed, cut, and punctured. To hold her crown in place, they drove a spike into the top of her head. Her cloud base was sawed in half.

Seeing that their precious statue had been so grossly scarred, the women of the parish rallied together. They took measurements, purchased fabrics, and stitched the finest clothing.

The women slipped a dainty, silk gown over her head and tenderly guided her remade, moveable arms into the sleeves. They covered her in a brocade mantle trimmed in gold. On her head, they placed a golden crown. By the time they had finished dressing the statue, it was likely that the women's eyes brimmed with tears. Our Lady looked like a Spanish Queen.

Although many colonists lived in poverty, Our Lady received generous gifts of dresses, capes, and jewelry from the Spanish settlers as well as the Indians. They all loved her.

However, they did not act lovingly toward each other. The Spaniards enslaved the Indians, forcing the men to haul huge logs and the women and children to make *adobe* bricks for the Christian churches. They were outraged that some Indians continued to practice their old rituals. The Spaniards called the Indians "heathens" and outlawed their religious rites, chants, and dances. They burned the *kivas,* underground chambers where the Indians held religious ceremonies.

In retaliation, the Indians killed a number of Spanish priests.

Prolonged drought, warring Apaches, and a shortage of supplies took a toll on both the Pueblo Indians and Spanish colonists. The Indians blamed the Christian god for not sending rain and blamed the Spanish priests for not allowing them to perform ceremonies and dances to bring rain. Indian medicine men who did perform rituals were charged with witchcraft and hanged.

Angry Indians banded together and devised a plan. Runners secretly delivered knotted yucca cords to each pueblo, with instructions to untie one knot per day until no knots were left on the cord, signifying the day for battle.

La Revuelta Indígena
The Indians Revolt

On August 10, 1680, the revolt began. Po'pay, a fearless leader from San Juan Pueblo, led 500 warring Indians in an attack on the colonists, burning their homes and killing entire families. The Indians killed priests at their altars and destroyed sacred symbols. About 400 Spaniards were killed, including 21 priests.

A young housewife, Josefa López Sambrano de Grijalva, remembered the treasured statue. She ran to the Church of the Immaculate Conception, which was in flames. With tears in her eyes, she snatched Our Lady from the altar and carried her to the Palace of the Governors where the colonists had taken refuge.

For the next ten days, the battle continued. The Spaniards killed 300 Indians, and many more were captured.

When the Indians cut off the water supply to the Palace of the Governors, the Spanish governor knew they were defeated. "We must leave immediately. Take only what you can carry."

Our Lady was, once again, taken over the same route she had traveled 55 years earlier—this time carried in the arms of a young woman. A portion of the journey was called *Jornada del Muerto*, Journey of the Dead Man, a grueling march through 90 miles of parched, sandy desert. There was no water, and August temperatures were extreme. Many colonists died from illness and exhaustion.

The Spanish colonists, along with a few converted Indians, eventually reached *El Paso del Norte*, which today is known as El Paso, Texas. For the next 12 years, the homeless colonists camped beside the *Rio del Norte*. For the cherished statue, they built a small church. Her clothing was simple—five dresses, four skirts, nine mantles, one black lace mantilla, and a few pair of earrings. The husband of Josefa Sambrano, the woman who had carried Our Lady so many miles to safety, gave Our Lady a crown and two new silk dresses.

The King of Spain was upset that the Indians had driven the colonists out of his kingdom. In 1692, he sent a nobleman, Don Diego de Vargas Zapata Luján Ponce de León, to reclaim *Nuevo México*.

**Don Diego de Vargas Zapata Luján Ponce de León.
Courtesy of Palace of the Governors.**

De Vargas visited 23 pueblos over a four-month period. In a gentle manner, he told the Indians that the Blessed Mother loved *both* the Indian and Spanish peoples and wanted them to live together peacefully. The Indians gave de Vargas a pledge of peace. When de Vargas entered Santa Fe in September 1692, his kind words were so convincing that the Indians released the colonists who had been held captive those past twelve years and agreed that the rest of the settlers could return.

Governor and Captain-General de Vargas declared his meeting with the Indians to be a peaceful reconquest and gave credit to the Virgin Mary for her help. De Vargas returned to *El Paso del Norte* with the good news. It was a time of rejoicing, and celebrations were held as far away as Mexico City.

In a letter to the Viceroy of New Spain dated January 12, 1693, de Vargas vowed to build a special chapel for "the patroness of said Kingdom and Villa . . . and to hold a yearly procession in her honor, her title being 'Our Lady of the Conquest.'"

Regresando a Casa
Returning Home

Once again, the statue—now *La Conquistadora*, Our Lady of the Conquest—rode in an oxcart over what was a familiar route, this time surrounded by a joyful crowd returning home. On October 4, 1693, the party of 100 soldiers, 70 families and 18 friars, along with horses, mules, and cattle, headed northward.

The journey took several months and the colonists arrived in the middle of winter on December 16, 1693. The weary travelers were excited. They were home. *La Conquistadora* was home. However, they were blocked from entering Santa Fe. The Indians had built a wall surrounding the capital so the colonists set up camp outside the city—and waited.

The Indians had changed their minds about welcoming home the Spanish settlers. Suppose de Vargas would not keep his word, and the Spaniards would mistreat them as they had before the revolt? The Indians refused to leave.

The colonists were *so* close to home, but forced to camp in bitter cold and blowing snow. From their place of safety, Indians taunted the Spaniards, calling out that their god could not save them from cold and hunger. The weary colonists pressured de Vargas to enforce the prior agreement so they could return to their homes.

They unpacked the statue and set up a makeshift altar in the middle of the camp. De Vargas knelt at the head of the colonists and prayed to *La Conquistadora* for her help in returning the colonists to their homes and promised to build her a suitable church.

On December 28, de Vargas issued the order for an assault. The Indians resisted, and a battle ensued. The Spaniards cut off the Indians' only water source, forcing the Indians to surrender. More than 70 Indians were killed and more than 400 taken captive.

By December 30, 1693, Santa Fe was, once again, under the control of Spain.

Believing that *La Conquistadora* had helped in returning the colonists to their homes, de Vargas donated a blue silk dress and a white mantel.

However, de Vargas struggled with dissension among his own people and with the Indians, and in July 1697, Don Pedro Cubero, became governor. He falsely accused de Vargas of wrongdoing in office and threw him in prison. Eventually, de Vargas was released and returned to Mexico City. After clearing his name, he was re-appointed as Governor of the Kingdom of *Nuevo México*. De Vargas returned in 1703, but died five months later before fulfilling his promise to build a church.

Finally, in 1714, faithful parishioners built a small adobe church with a special chapel for *La Conquistadora*. At last, she had a permanent home.

Governor General Don Diego de Vargas, as well as Father Benavides, would have been pleased that the humble wooden statue, once exiled, was now enthroned as the Queen of New Mexico in her own chapel at the Cathedral of St. Francis of Assisi in the heart of New Mexico.

The Old Parroquia about 1865. Photograph by Nicholas Brown.
Courtesy of Palace of the Governors.

In 1886, construction of a new cathedral began. Walls were built surrounding the original adobe church and atop the remains of four earlier churches. Portions of the smaller building were torn down and carried out through the massive cathedral doors. However, *La Conquistadora*'s chapel, the side chapel, was preserved.

The ornate cathedral was designed using three styles of architecture: adobe, French-Romanesque, and modern, with stained-glass windows from France. Stones for the main structure were quarried from south of Santa Fe, an area now named after Archbishop Lamy.

Santa Fe continued to attract settlers, many of whom traveled the long, dusty trail called the *Camino Real de Tierra Adentro* or Royal Road of the Interior. The 1600-mile long trail ran from Mexico City to *San Juan de los Caballeros*, just north of Santa Fe. Once a network of footpaths connecting indigenous people, the trade route accommodated mule trains and oxcarts carrying supplies.

One campsite on the historic *El Camino Real* was *El Rancho de las Golondrinas,* the last stopping place before reaching Santa Fe.

El Rancho de las Golondrinas is a living museum that portrays Spanish colonial life in the 1700s. The historic ranch consists of original colonial outbuildings as well as historic structures.

Covered entrance to courtyard of Spanish colonial home.
Photo by Larry Greenly. Courtesy of *El Rancho de las Golondrinas.*

Courtyard of colonial home, well, horno, and chapel.
Photo by Larry Greenly. Courtesy of *El Rancho de las Golondrinas.*

Hornos (outdoor ovens).
Photo by Larry Greenly. Courtesy of *El Rancho de las Golondrinas.*

Corral of churro sheep.
Photo by Larry Greenly. Courtesy of *El Rancho de las Golondrinas.*

Oxcarts.
Photo by Larry Greenly. Courtesy of *El Rancho de las Golondrinas.*

Spanish hacienda.
Photo by Larry Greenly. Courtesy of *El Rancho de las Golondrinas.*

Historic outbuilding.
Photo by Larry Greenly. Courtesy of *El Rancho de las Golondrinas.*

Outbuilding.
Photo by Larry Greenly. Courtesy of *El Rancho de las Golondrinas.*

Historic church.
Photo by Larry Greenly. Courtesy of *El Rancho de las Golondrinas.*

Cemetery and church.
Photo by Larry Greenly. Courtesy of *El Rancho de las Golondrinas.*

Historic mill.
Photo by Larry Greenly. Courtesy of *El Rancho de las Golondrinas.*

La Restauración
The Restoration

The years took their toll on *La Conquistadora*. She had been disfigured by the hacking and sawing of amateur woodcutters, as well as being frequently dressed and undressed. By 1930, her face, formed from a type of plaster called gesso and layered in paint, was beginning to crumble. Some of her fingers had broken off.

Gustave Baumann, a German artist and masterful carver of marionettes, took on the task of restoring the statue to her original grandeur. Her wooden body and head had been carved with delicate details, never intended to be dressed in fabrics. The original carved locks of hair framing her face had been cut and scraped and replaced with a wig.

La Conquistadora before Gustave Baumann restoration. Photograph by T. Harmon Parkhurst. Courtesy of Palace of the Governors.

Baumann repaired the base, which had been cut in half. He mended her mutilated knee and carved several new fingers. Then he skillfully refined her delicate facial features. Gustave Baumann restored her natural beauty, her dignity, and her poise.

Baumann also carved a replica of *La Conquistadora* known as *La Peregrina,* the pilgrim. Her home is at Rosario Chapel, but she frequently travels to other churches.

By the late 1990s, the base of the statue was deteriorating. During its next restoration, artist Mark Humenick discovered the wooden statue had a hollow core, which, most likely, enabled her to be carried on a pole. He sent a piece of wood to the University of Arizona, and experts there concluded the statue had been carved between 1448 and 1648, leading to the assumption the statue came from Spain to Mexico.

A dendrologist at the University of Cincinnati examined a sliver of wood from behind the ear of the statue and concluded that she was carved from willow wood. However, during the later restoration, wood shavings from the statue's back were privately analyzed and determined to be olive wood. How could she be carved from both willow wood and olive wood? Only *La Conquistadora* knows.

Nombres Nuevos
New Names

La Conquistadora was proclaimed "Patroness of Nuevo México and Queen of Heaven" in 1771 by the *La Cofradía de La Conquistadora*.

In 1960, she was named "Queen and Patroness of the ancient kingdom of New Mexico and of its villa of Santa Fe" at a Papal coronation attended by thousands of people honoring Santa Fe's 350th anniversary. An apostolic representative of Pope John XXIII honored *La Conquistadora* with the *Corona Grande*, or Papal Crown, a 14-carat gold crown set with a three-carat diamond and many precious stones.

Archbishop Robert Sanchez of Santa Fe gave *La*

Conquistadora an additional title: *Nuestra Señora de la Paz*, or "Our Lady of Peace." Her new name, given to her in 1992, was an effort "to heal all hurts of the past and to bring all people together, uniting them with her conquering love."

In 2005, Pope Benedict XVI designated the cathedral as a basilica: The Cathedral Basilica of St. Francis of Assisi.

La Capilla de La Conquistadora
La Conquistadora Chapel

Today, *La Conquistadora* reigns in splendor from her throne in the La Conquistadora Chapel, a side chapel in the Cathedral Basilica of St. Francis of Assisi. She is surrounded by the warm glow of candles, the fragrance of fresh flowers, and the music of rehearsing choirs.

On the east wall is a stained glass window depicting Archbishop John Baptiste Lamy, New Mexico's first archbishop. Underneath is a burial vault containing the bones of two early Franciscan priests.

The chapel underwent major renovations when Pope Pius XII declared 1954 a Marian year, and *La Conquistadora* was crowned by Cardinal Francis

Spellman of New York. To mark the occasion, a Spanish altar screen made from two 18th century side altars was installed.

The La Conquistadora Chapel. Photograph by Larry Greenly.

A *sacristana*, a person who acts in an official capacity to care for sacred items, maintains *La Conquistadora's* chapel and oversees her elaborate wardrobe. The duties of this highly respected position are performed as a devotion to the Blessed Mother. On occasion, family members assist the *sacristana* with the cleaning and maintenance of the chapel, considered to be a sacred family experience.

La Conquistadora receives thousands of guests per year. Some come out of curiosity, but many bring their burdens to this statue who represents the Mother of Jesus. In the quiet and still presence of the Blessed Mother, visitors light candles and kneel in prayer. Some leave behind their prayers, which they write in a notebook that rests on a lectern at the chapel entrance.

A visitor reported that the reverence of the chapel gave her a sense of peace and calmness; another felt her heart opening to love and compassion. One woman from out of town had received a court summons to settle a legal issue. She shared her anxieties with a local shopkeeper and asked for the name of a psychic. Instead, the shopkeeper referred her to *La Conquistadora*. The next day, the shopkeeper received flowers with a note stating that the sender had paid a visit to *La Conquistadora* and the legal matters had been resolved in the woman's favor.

People from all over the world are drawn to this humble statue whose own story is filled with triumphs and tragedies.

El Guardarropa y las Joyas de la Reina
The Queen's Wardrobe and Jewelry

Regardless of what the cherished statue is wearing, *La Conquistadora* is clothed with love. She may be Santa Fe's best-dressed lady, with a wardrobe of more than 200 dresses made of fabrics from around the world.

The *sacristana* changes *La Conquistadora's* attire at the beginning of each month, on holidays, and on special occasions. Dressing the 30-inch statue takes one to two hours, during which time the *sacristana* prays for herself and for others.

Sewing for the Blessed Mother has been said to be a spiritual experience. The seamstresses believe Our

Lady has the power to perform miracles, and they work reverently. They often sew written prayers or intentions into the seams of the garments. Some dresses are sewn as gestures of gratitude for answered prayers. Others have connections to historical celebrations. Each gown has a story to tell in cloth, thread, and devotion.

Design on scapular of the ensemble made to commemorate the ordination of Father Jerome. Photograph by Larry Greenly.

When The Reverend Monsignor Jerome Martinez, the current pastor of the Cathedral Basilica of St. Francis of Assisi, was ordained in 1976, his mother, Nelda Martinez, sewed an outfit for *La Conquistadora*. The ensemble is made of eggshell-colored cotton fabric with a Southwestern turquoise and black design down the front of the scapular. The same design adorns the back of the cape.

**Back of cape made to commemorate the ordination of Father Jerome.
Photograph by Larry Greenly.**

One seamstress, Julia Gómez, said she had contemplated for years what type of dress she could make, but nothing came to her. When Ms. Gómez learned to weave, she felt the statue speak to her, saying "Make me one of these dresses. I don't have one." So Ms. Gómez designed a traditional Spanish dress that took more than a year to make. She sheared sheep and spun the wool fleece into yarn that she wove into fabric. She then colored the fabric with natural dyes from flowers, vegetables, and roots, and embroidered it using a *colcha* stitch. This intricate embroidery stitch is a relatively lost art but was common in the 1600s when women embroidered flowers or birds to adorn bedcovers, altar cloths, and garments. Now, Our Lady could be appropriately dressed for Spanish Market weekend.

Colcha stitch design details. Photograph by Roger Blake.

Colcha stitch design details. Photograph by Roger Blake.

Colcha ensemble. Photograph by Roger Blake.

For a liturgy during Indian Market weekend, Dorothy Trujillo from Cochiti Pueblo created a pueblo-style outfit for Our Lady—a traditional *manta*, a dress made of heavy black fabric with red and green lines stitched across the top and a woven red and green sash. Her daughter, Judy, made a white manta.

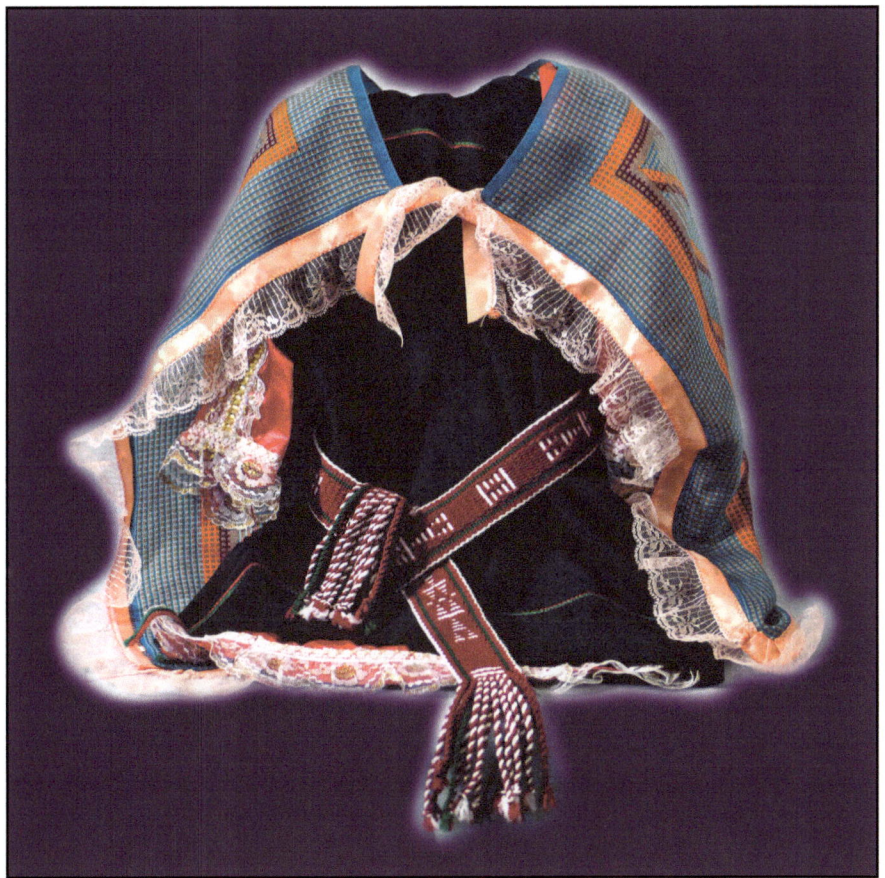

Cochiti *Manta*. Photograph by Roger Blake.

Cochiti *Manta*. Photograph by Roger Blake.

Onofre Trujillo, Dorothy's husband, hand-crafted a miniature squash blossom necklace, silver bracelet, and rings.

A seamstress and former *sacristana*, Mary Martinez-Dean of Santa Fe, made a fiesta dress for Our Lady to wear during the Santa Fe Fiesta. The turquoise satin dress has a gathered, tiered skirt trimmed in rows of silver rickrack made from the woman's own childhood fiesta dress.

Fiesta Dress. Photograph by Roger Blake.

After her mother's death, Ms. Martinez-Dean said she had a dream in which she saw elegant blue fabric with golden threads. She believed the Blessed Mother was asking for a dress to be made from this cloth, but Ms. Martinez-Dean could not find the material she had seen in her dream. Sometime later, she visited the site of Mary's appearance in Fatima, Portugal. There, in a shop selling religious items, was the exact fabric that had appeared in her dream. Although a bus was waiting to take her to the airport, she could not leave without purchasing the fabric. The bus driver was annoyed, but he waited and did get her to the airport in time. When she returned home, she sewed the dress and a beaded scapular.

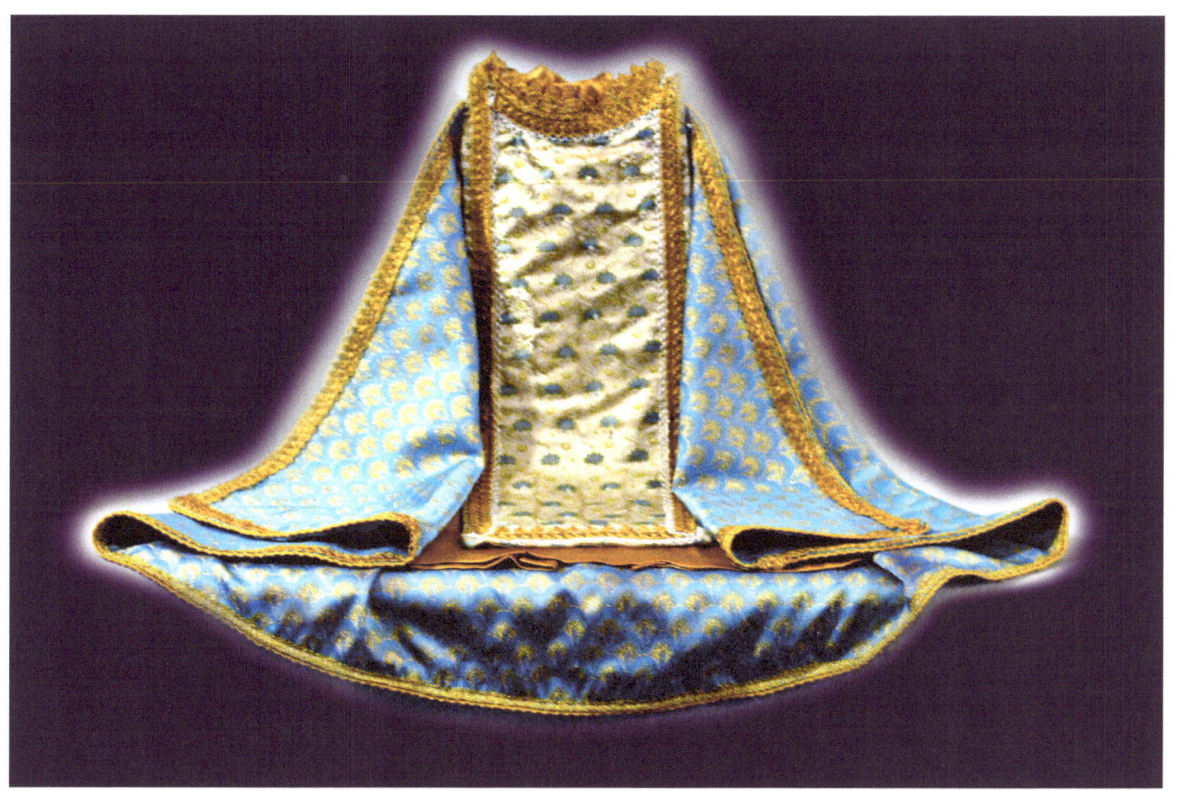

Fatima Dress. Photograph by Roger Blake.

Sixteen-year-old Jennifer Apodaca from Las Vegas, Nevada, followed a family custom of sewing for the statue. With the help of her mother, she made a purple satin dress for Lent. The black lace overlay represented Mary mourning the death of her son.

On wintry days in the high desert of Santa Fe, Our Lady might wear an ermine cape. This beautiful cape was donated by Franciscan priests from Holy Cross, Alaska.

One woman, whose mother was very ill, asked God to give her mother another year of life and promised to have a special dress made for Our Lady. Her mother did live another year, and the woman kept her promise to have a special dress made. The *sacristana* invited the woman to dress Our Lady in the new blue gown. As the woman dressed the statue, her eyes overflowed with tears while her father sat in a rocking chair, praying.

Paul Valdez loves the history surrounding the statue. He grew up in his grandmother's bridal shop and, when he was only 15, he began sewing for the Blessed Mother. Ali McGraw, a movie star who lives in Santa Fe, commissioned Mr. Valdez to make a gown for *La Conquistadora*. The sienna-colored, silk brocade organza gown with gold-thread designs is edged with a pleated white chiffon ruffle. A small charm depicting the image of St. Joseph is sewn on the edge of the hem. Underneath the skirt, a closed pocket holds a written prayer.

The Ali McGraw Dress. Photograph by Roger Blake.

Some of Our Lady's elegant garments might be considered hand-me-downs.

Several dresses are made from wedding gowns. One dress was made from a scapular that had belonged to a statue of the Virgin Mary in Guatemala.

Fray Angélico Chávez, a noted New Mexico historian who had been a chaplain in World War II, had a mantle, or cloak, made from his military uniform. This mantle was made to express gratitude to the Mother of God for the end of the war.

Another mantle came from the Blessed Sacrament cape that once belonged to Archbishop Lamy. The cape was discovered in a crypt beneath the cathedral where the archbishop is buried. The gorgeous mantle made for Our Lady has gold-threaded French embroidery decorated with red and purple flowers.

Just as mortal women sometimes change their minds about what they are going to wear, Our Lady also has preferences. A former *sacristana,* Emelda Martinez-Garcia, reported that during one December she tried to dress Our Lady in the same gown she had worn the past three Christmases. It appeared the dress did not fit. After an hour, she put the Christmas gown away and brought out Our Lady's white birthday dress. The dainty lace gown trimmed in pearls and baby roses slipped easily over the statue's head. Tears came to Ms. Martinez-Garcia's eyes when she saw the gown was almost identical to her sister Irene's wedding dress. Ms.

Martinez-Garcia said that Our Lady, herself, chose the white birthday dress to wear for Christmas.

One man reported that, on occasion, when he is sewing for *La Conquistadora*, the material bunches up and tangles the machine threads. He believes this to be an indication the statue does not approve of the fabric.

Our Lady has a priceless collection of jewelry. In addition to earrings, bracelets, and necklaces suitable for every outfit, Our Lady also has a selection of crowns. One gold crown is studded with precious stones, including a three-carat diamond. Another tiara-style sterling silver crown, inlaid with turquoise and a miniature gold cross, was made by David Griego with the help of his son. Mr. Griego stated that, after this endeavor, his relationship with his son became closer and his business flourished.

La Conquistadora also has a very expensive necklace: a cross made of gold, diamonds, sapphires, and emeralds. This exquisite piece of jewelry mysteriously arrived in the daily mail. The plain envelope was addressed to "La Conquistadora" with no return address. She wears this cross during processions and other special occasions.

On occasion, Our Lady is seen with the Baby Jesus cradled in her arms. He has a wardrobe that matches some of his Blessed Mother's. This six-inch replica of a baby boy has scraped knees as many boys do. He sometimes wears booties or tiny gold sandals.

Baby Jesus. Photograph by Roger Blake.

El Secuestro
The Kidnapping

La Conquistadora maintained a quiet presence at the cathedral. Then, early on March 18, 1973, the church custodian made a shocking discovery. He immediately telephoned the police. "*La Conquistadora* is missing!"

Police arrived to find the cathedral doors locked and no broken windows. They searched under benches and in the balconies. Muddy footprints were found around the altar and outside the church, but there was no Madonna. Detectives concluded that the thief had hidden inside the cathedral, waited until everyone left, and then stole the statue. Police combed the busy streets and dark alleys. Across the country, people asked, "Who would take a cherished sacred statue?"

Church bells rang out across the city. The mayor declared a "Day of Mourning," and the city fell silent. People grieved the loss and prayed for her return. A reward was offered.

On April 7th, a priest at the cathedral received an envelope, which he opened carefully. It contained the cross from *La Conquistadora's* crown along with a letter. In poorly written Italian, the sender demanded:

> *Give us $150,000 in cash and promise no legal punishment in exchange for the return of the statue. If you will agree to this, someone should ring the cathedral bells ten times at 4:45 p.m. on Wednesday. You will receive more instructions.*

Church bells tolled as the thief instructed, but phone lines were silent. Finally, one evening, the telephone rang. Detectives traced the call to the home of a young boy. When police confronted him, he confessed and told them the name of his accomplice.

The boy led police to the Manzano Mountains, over 100 miles from Santa Fe. There, in an old mine shaft, they found *La Conquistadora* wrapped in plastic. She was still wearing a bright red gown and holding a crystal rosary, but her golden crown was missing.

Days later, the crown was found buried in an arroyo.

La Conquistadora's return called for a celebration, but the statue was locked away in the evidence room of the Santa Fe Police Department. Devoted followers anxiously waited. Two weeks later, several thousand people gathered at city hall for a procession to the cathedral. Church bells rang joyously as police and city attorneys carried *La Conquistadora* through the streets while 65 children from a first communion class showered her with flowers. The cathedral resonated with prayers of thanksgiving.

La Fiesta de Santa Fe
The Santa Fe Fiesta

The Santa Fe Fiesta is reported to be the oldest continual community celebration in the United States, having been established by the 1712 Proclamation of the Santa Fe Fiesta Council. The historic decree was drafted by Santa Fe city officials establishing a fiesta "recalling how this Villa had been reconquered on September 14, 1692 . . . and be celebrated with vespers, mass, sermon and procession."

On the eve of the fiesta, crowds gather at Fort Marcy Park for the burning of Zozobra or "Old Man Gloom," a 50-foot marionette made of wood, paper, and fabrics. Through the burning of Zozobra, people release their "glooms" (worries and troubles) from the past year.

Zozobra or Old Man Gloom at Santa Fe Fiesta. Photograph by New Mexico State Tourist Bureau. Courtesy of Palace of the Governors.

The three-day event in September consists of music, dancing, and ceremonies with a costumed de Vargas and Queen. For the popular Pet Parade, pets as well as their owners and children dress in costumes and parade around the plaza.

The fiesta ends with a mass of thanksgiving at the Cathedral Basilica of St. Francis of Assisi followed by a half-mile candlelight procession to the Cross of the Martyrs. Here, on a hill dotted with sagebrush at the base of the Sangre de Cristo Mountains, a white cross stands overlooking the city. A metal plaque bears the names of the 21 priests murdered during the 1680 Pueblo Revolt.

Cross of the Martyrs. Photograph by Larry Greenly.

La Procesión a Rosario
Procession to Rosario

$\mathcal{J}$ust as de Vargas promised in 1693, *La Conquistadora* is taken in procession every year on the Sunday following Corpus Christi, nine Sundays after Easter. The tradition is a solemn display of gratitude for *La Conquistadora's* help in returning the colonists to Santa Fe.

Cathedral bells ring boldly across Santa Fe. Under New Mexico's bluest skies, burning incense mingles with the singing of sacred songs. In orderly fashion, parishioners file through the massive bronze doors and down the steps of the Cathedral Basilica of St. Francis of Assisi.

**Cathedral Basilica of St. Francis of Assisi, 2010.
Photograph by Larry Greenly.**

The masters of ceremony lead the pilgrimage, which includes incense bearers and priests carrying lighted candles. An ancient Spanish flag, gold with red zigzag streaks, heralds the royalty—those portraying Governor and Captain-General Don Diego de Vargas, the Fiesta Queen, and her court. Parishioners from neighboring churches carry colorful banners and recite prayers.

The choir sings hymns and children sprinkle rose petals before the Caballeros de Vargas. These gentlemen are strikingly dressed in white satin shirts, black pants, and red cummerbunds. They take turns shouldering a platform that carries the regal-looking statue.

In early years, it was the women of the confraternity who carried the statue. They stopped at intervals where the statue was placed on a temporary pedestal and prayers were offered.

La Conquistadora procession outside St. Francis Cathedral.
Photograph by H.H. Dorman. Courtesy of Palace of the Governors.

Today, the crowd swells as more participants merge with the procession. Families with strollers, elderly people carrying umbrellas, tattooed teenagers clad in low-slung jeans, and even a padre in a black robe and white surplice wearing a Rockies baseball cap reverently file past closed stores and police cars blocking traffic.

Everyone strains for a glimpse of the elegantly dressed statue being carried through the narrow, winding streets of Santa Fe. The procession spills onto the wide North Guadalupe Street and turns through the well-kept cemetery.

The one mile, 50-minute procession finally reaches the Rosario Chapel, the site where the colonists camped outside Santa Fe more than 300 years ago.

Rosario Chapel and St. Catherine's Indian School about 1890.
Photograph by Dana B. Chase. Courtesy of Palace of the Governors.

Rosario Chapel in 2011. Photograph by Larry Greenly.

Stained glass windows invite the afternoon sun. Bells begin to ring, softer than the large cathedral bells—but clear and crisp, welcoming the statue.

Inside the humble chapel, people kneel on the bare, tiled floor, continuing to pray and sing hymns while *La Conquistadora* is positioned on the altar.

Her week-long presence at Rosario is a time of renewal, prayer, and thanksgiving. Daily masses are part of a novena of devotional masses, which may be attended by as many as three and four generations of a family. The following Sunday, *La Conquistadora* returns to the cathedral where the novena will be completed.

After a benediction, a guitarist accompanies the congregation in a soulful song:

> *Adiós Reina del cielo,*
> *Madre del Salvador.*
> *Adiós, O Madre mía,*
> *Adiós, adiós, adiós.*

> Farewell, O Queen of Heaven,
> Mother of Our Savior.
> Goodbye, Mother,
> Farewell, farewell, farewell.

La Conquistadora and Child at Rosario Chapel. Photograph by Robert Martin. Courtesy of Palace of the Governors.

Bibliography

Abreu, Margaret. "The Little Lights." *New Mexico Magazine*. December, 1959.

Bial, Raymond. *The Pueblo*. New York: Marshall Cavendish, 2000.

Casey, Robert L. *Journey to the High Southwest, A Traveler's Guide*. Guilford, Connecticut: The Globe Pequot Press, 1983.

Chavez, Fray Angelico. *La Conquistadora: The Autobiography of an Ancient Statue*. Santa Fe, New Mexico: Sunstone Press, 1975.

Chavez, Fray Angelico. "La Conquistadora–Her 350th Anniversary." *New Mexico Magazine,* September, 1975.

Chavez, Fray Angelico. *Our Lady of the Conquest*. Santa Fe, New Mexico: Sunstone Press. New Edition, 2010.

Chevalier, Jaima. *La Conquistadora*. Santa Fe, New Mexico. Sunstone Press, 2010.

Drabanski, Emily. "Ancient Statue's Attire Made with Devotion." *New Mexico Magazine*. September, 1992.

"El Camino Real de Tierra Adentro National Historic Trail." www.blm.gov/.../etc./.../caminoreal. (accessed 2010 November 10)

Gallegos, Ronald. "La Conquistadora Stolen From Church." *The New Mexican*. March 19, 1973, Section A.

——"Conquistadora Search Widens." *The New Mexican*. March 20 1973, Section A.

——"Conquistadora Probe Continues." *The New Mexican*. March 22,1973, Section A.

——"A Day of Mourning." *The New Mexican*. March 25, 1973, Section A.

——"Santa Fe Officials Release Conquistadora, Other Art." *The New Mexican*. April 29, 1973, Section A.

——"La Conquistadora Recovered: 2 Suspects Held; Items Safe." *The New Mexican*. April 15, 1973, Section A.

——"SF Sets 'day of Madonna,' " *The New Mexican*. April 16, 1973, Section A.

——"Searchers Unable to Find Crown." *The New Mexican*. April 17, 1973, Section A.

Harbert, Nancy. *New Mexico*. Oakland, California: Compass American Guides, 1992.

"The History of Conquistadora." *The New Mexican*. March 25, 1973, Section A.

"The History of the Santa Fe Fiesta." www.santafefiesta.org/history.html. (accessed 2007 July 23).

Maldonado, Jim. "Agenda Details Released for Conquistadora Fiesta." *The New Mexican*. April 20, 1973, Section A.

——"Patroness Returns," *The New Mexican*. April 30, 1973, Section A.

Martinez, Rev. Jerome. "Our Lady of Conquering Love." sermon, n.d.

McLaughlin, Judith. *Sacred Feminine*. Albuquerque, New Mexico: Rio Grande Books, 2009.

Preston, Douglas and Jose Antonio Esquibel. *The Royal Road.* Albuquerque: University of New Mexico Press, 1998.

Ribera-Ortega, Pedro. "La Conquistadora: America's Oldest Madonna." Santa Fe, New Mexico: Sunstone Press, 1975.

Roberts, Susan A., and Calvin A. Roberts. *A History of New Mexico.* Albuquerque: University of New Mexico Press, 2002.

"Searchers Find Crown, Old Frames." *The New Mexican.* April 18, 1973, Section A.

Simmons, Marc. *New Mexico!* Albuquerque: University of New Mexico Press, 1993.

Weigle, Marta, and Peter White. *The Lore of New Mexico.* Albuquerque: University of New Mexico Press, 1988.

www.ingramcontent.com/pod-product-compliance
Lightning Source LLC
Chambersburg PA
CBHW041540220426
43663CB00003B/86